9.84

EVANSTON PUBLIC LIBRARY

P9-CQW-838

x597.9 Switz.M

Switzer, Merebeth.

Turtles /

DATE DUE

MAR 1 4 2003	
JUN 2 6 2003	JUL 1 5 2004
	MAY 2 9 2004
OCT 1 9 2003	AUG 2 6 2004
DEC 1 6 2003	
	JAN 5 - 2005
	AUG 1 8 2005
FEB 8 2004	
FEB 2 9 2004	
APR 0 2 2004	
JUL 1 5 2004	

DEMCO, INC. 38-2931

Nature's Children

TURTLES

Merebeth Switzer

Grolier

EVANSTON PUBLIC LIBRARY
CHILDREN'S DEPARTMENT
1703 ORRINGTON AVENUE
EVANSTON, ILLINOIS 60201

FACTS IN BRIEF

Classification of North American turtles

    Class: *Reptilia* (reptiles)

    Order: *Testudines*

    Family: Seven main families; the largest in North America is *Emydidae* (family of sub-aquatic turtles) which contains eight genera and 26 species.

    Genus: 19 genera of turtles are found in North America.

    Species: There are approximately 50 North American species.

World distribution.   Varies with species.

Habitat.   Varies with species.

Distinctive physical characteristics.   Protective shell covers body; hard toothless beak.

Habits.   Lay their eggs on land, most bury them.

Diet.   Varies with species.

Published originally as
"Getting to Know . . . Nature's Children."

This series is approved and recommended by the Federation of Ontario Naturalists.

This library reinforced edition is available exclusively from:

Grolier Educational Corporation
Sherman Turnpike, Danbury, Connecticut 06816

Copyright © 1986 by Grolier Limited. All rights reserved.

Contents

If you could look back in time and see the earth as it appeared 200 million years ago, what would you see? Giant trees, strange plants and dinosaurs. But look, what's that? Why it's a turtle. That's right, there were turtles way back in the days of the dinosaurs. And, amazingly, they have changed very little since that time.

Maybe that is why turtles have fascinated people and why there are so many stories and legends about them. You almost certainly know at least one turtle story: Aesop's fable about the Tortoise that races the Hare—and wins! But did you know that ancient legends from places as far apart as China, North America and India say that the earth is carried on the back of a turtle?

Do turtles deserve the reputation for slowness and dependability that stories and legends give them? And how did they survive so much longer than their ancient friends?

Wood Turtle.

Wise Young Turtles

Imagine a long, wide stretch of empty beach. It is the middle of the night, but the moon and stars are out.

Look over there, where the sand meets the trees. Can you see that place where the sand seems to be moving? Watch carefully now. . . isn't that a little dark spot, just there? It's moving this way, toward the water . . . . And there's another one behind it and another.

What can they be, these tiny crawling shapes coming up out of the sand?

They are turtle hatchlings. But where do they come from, and where are they going? And why are these babies out here alone?

One of the truly amazing things about turtles is that they are born knowing almost everything they need to know to cope with the world on their own. Once their mother has prepared their nest, laid her eggs and covered them carefully, she has done all she needs to do for her babies.

And that is only ONE of the amazing things . . . .

Opposite page:

These newly hatched Painted Turtles will not reach their full size until they are five years old. In the wild they may live up to 20 years.

Reptile Relatives

Turtles are reptiles. This means they are relatives of crocodiles, snakes and lizards. All reptiles have certain features in common. For one thing, although some spend a great deal of time in the water, they must breathe air, just as you do.

What else do reptiles have in common? Well, think carefully: have you ever seen a furry snake or a turtle with eyelashes? No? That is because reptiles do not have hair. Instead they have a thick scaly or leathery covering.

Finally, reptiles have no built-in temperature control. While your body stays at more or less the same temperature no matter how cold or hot the weather, a reptile's does not. Its temperature will go up when it is in the sun and down when it moves into the shade.

As you can imagine, this affects how and where reptiles, including turtles, live.

Opposite page:

Often all you see of the Spiny Softshell Turtle is the tip of its snout sticking above the water!

Turtle Territory

Turtles are found almost anywhere that it is warm for at least several months of the year. Although they depend on their surroundings to keep their body at the right temperature, they have ways of surviving winters. But in between they need a good period of summer warmth and sunshine.

In North America this means that turtles can live all through the United States and Mexico but only in the southern part of Canada. Some types, such as the Painted and Snapping Turtles, are found in many regions. Others— the Yellow Blotch Map Turtle, for instance— are found only in one small area.

The Eastern Painted Turtle, though common, is shy and difficult to approach.

What's in a Name?

You have probably heard someone call turtles tortoises. And you may have run into yet another name—terrapin.

Fortunately, this is not really as confusing as it may seem. There are many different kinds of turtles, but they fall into three main categories: sea turtles, tortoises or land turtles, and freshwater turtles, sometimes called terrapins.

Whatever they are are called, they are all turtles.

Who's Who

Sea turtles are found in the Atlantic and Pacific oceans and in the Gulf of Mexico. Their legs are flattened, paddle-like flippers and they spend almost all their time in the water. They only come ashore to lay their eggs. Most sea turtles are very large. Many grow to be over 100 kilograms (220 pounds).

Tortoises are turtles that can live only on land. They are are poor swimmers and usually live near deserts and grasslands. You can recognize them by their stump-like legs and their high, rounded shells.

Although some turtles spend their entire lives on land, most spend part of their time in the water and part on land. The turtles you probably know best are the freshwater turtles you might find near your home or cottage or on special country outings. These turtles spend part of their time in the water of lakes, ponds and streams and part on land. They have many different styles of shells and their feet are usually suited for both walking and swimming. Most of these turtles have claws, and some of those that spend a great deal of time in the water have webbed feet.

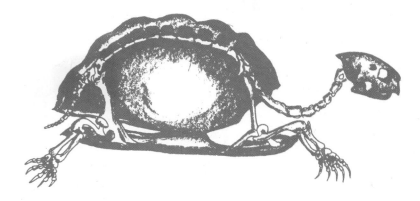

The turtle's shell is part of its body. It is very firmly attached and the turtle could not survive without it.

Built-in Armor

If you were asked to describe a turtle, where would you start? With its shell, of course. After all, to most of us, that is what makes a turtle a turtle.

Turtle shells can look very different, however. They may be high and rounded like that of the tortoise; or low and sleek and streamlined for gliding through water. Or any style in between.

Turtle shells may be brown or green all over or a mottled mixture of dullish shades. Or they may have brightly colored spots, streaks and borders or intricate patterns.

But whatever a turtle's shell looks like, it is bony and hard and it is the turtle's main means of protection. Many turtles can pull their head, tail and legs inside their shell— and they do so at the first hint of danger.

This built-in armor may be one of the reasons that turtles have survived for so many generations.

Opposite page:

The faint yellow lines on its shell give the Map Turtle its name.

A Box Turtle has a large hinged plastron and can withdraw completely into its shell.

Snapping Turtles have very small plastrons and cannot pull their head and legs inside.

Opposite page:

Blanding's Turtle.

Upside/Downside

A turtle's shell is made up of two parts—a top called the carapace and a bottom called the plastron. The parts are usually joined at the sides by bony ridges. At the front and back ends are openings through which the turtle's head, tail and chunky legs stick out.

Both parts of the turtle's shell have an inner layer made up of bony plates that are actually part of the turtle's backbone and ribs. Covering this on most turtles is a layer of broad, thin scales called scutes. These are made of material something like your fingernails.

Sometimes a turtle may have sharp points on its back or other strange looking lumps. These are scutes that are specially built to help it blend into its surroundings or to make it look threatening.

Some turtles shed their scutes as they grow. But new ones are already formed underneath, so this does not leave the turtle without protection.

Stinky Stinkpot

Most grown-up turtles have shells that are strong enough to keep them pretty safe. Babies, however, and some other turtles are so small that their shell does not pose much of a problem for predators.

But some small turtles have another special safety device. The Stinkpot and its close relatives the Mud and Musk Turtles have two glands that produce a strong smelly liquid called musk. When they are disturbed, they release this unpleasant musk all over the intruder. A close encounter with a Stinkpot will show you that its name is well deserved!

The Stinkpot may be small but its smell is mighty.

Clumsy on Land

Turtles are famous for their slowness and it is true that most of them move slowly and awkwardly on land.

Strangely enough, tortoises—the turtles that live entirely on land—move particularly clumsily on their stumpy legs and small feet. No wonder Aesop's Hare thought it had nothing to worry about in its race with the Tortoise!

Freshwater turtles move more quickly on land than most tortoises. Some can even run (though not what you would call *fast*), and some can climb. The Stinkpot, for example, can climb the trunks of small trees to a height of more than two metres (6 feet).

Nonetheless, most freshwater and all sea turtles move most easily in the water. They can swim quite quickly and large sea turtles can cover great distances. They may migrate hundreds of kilometres (miles) to find food or to return to the nesting sites where they hatched to lay their own eggs.

Opposite page:

The Green Sea Turtle has been known to stay underwater for up to five hours.

Lung Power

A turtle breathes through its mouth and nose and uses lungs, just as you do. However, it does have one difficulty.

If you place your hand on your chest you will feel your ribs moving, helping you to breathe. The turtle's ribs, being fixed to its shell, cannot move. But the turtle's body is specially built so that it can make its lungs expand simply by moving its legs.

Many turtles spend a great deal of their time underwater. They still need to breathe. Some have ways for their bodies to take small amounts of oxygen directly from the water. Others have a long, snorkel-like nose that allows them to keep their body underwater while they breathe oxygen from the air. And all of them can slow down their heartbeat when they are underwater, so that their body needs less oxygen. How long they can stay underwater without coming up for air depends on the kind of turtle—and on what it is doing. A swimming turtle uses up oxygen much faster than a resting one.

Opposite page:

Taking a breather. (Blanding's Turtle)

Turtle Senses

Turtles do not have the same kind of ears as you. A turtle's ears are flat against its head and are really pieces of skin stretched over the ear opening. People used to think that turtles could not hear sounds but could only feel them through their body. We now know that a turtle can actually hear as well as a cat, and some owners of pet turtles claim that their pet will come when they call.

Turtles see quite well too. Unlike many animals they can see colors and seem to be particularly sensitive to red. And unlike their cousins the snakes, turtles have moveable eyelids and can blink.

Don't worry if you see a turtle gulping air. It is not having trouble breathing. It is simply bringing air into its mouth in order to smell its surroundings and sniff out its next meal.

The Box Turtle can pull itself completely inside its shell and close itself tightly into a nearly enemy-proof box.

Turtle Treats

And speaking of meals, what do turtles like to eat? That depends on the type of turtle and the kinds of food available.

Some types of turtles, especially the tortoises, feed mainly on plants. They are called herbivores. Other types eat only meat. They are called carnivores. The Snapping Turtle is a carnivore. It feeds on insects, crayfish, crabs, snails, fish, frogs, toads, snakes, birds' eggs and small mammals.

Most turtles, however, are omnivores, which means they will eat anything. They do have favorite foods though, and so we are fairly sure they have a keen sense of taste. The Leatherback, for example, has a definite passion for jellyfish, while the Green Sea Turtle eats only eel grass.

Most turtles can go for days or even weeks without eating. But when food is plentiful, they will eat all they can and may become quite fat.

Opposite page:

To avoid the hot sun the Desert Tortoise feeds in the early morning or late afternoon.

Toothless Jaws and Tempting Tongues

To munch all this food you would think that a turtle must have a pretty good set of teeth. This is not the case. In fact, turtles have no teeth at all! They do, however, have a hard beak which has a rough cutting edge that they use to tear apart and sometimes grind their food. Some turtles, such as the Alligator Snapping Turtle, have such a strong beak that they could easily cut a fish in half—and possibly chomp off a finger. With all Snapping Turtles, it is best to let an expert handle them.

A turtle cannot stick out its tongue, but it does have one. It uses its tongue to move food around in its mouth and into its throat. The Alligator Snapping Turtle even has an extra tongue-like growth in its mouth that looks rather like a worm. When the turtle holds its mouth open and wiggles this, it acts like a fishing lure. Soon an unwary fish swims in expecting dinner. Instead, the fish becomes dinner for the turtle.

Opposite page:

A Snapping Turtle cannot hide inside its shell. If attacked it must defend itself, and this may be why it has a reputation for being aggressive. Actually, it will slip away rather than fight if it can.

Turtle Talk

Turtles are basically quiet creatures. They live pretty much on their own, and most of them do not have special areas they protect from other turtles. This means that they really have little need to communicate with each other.

Turtles do make sounds, however. Some may grunt and others have a whistling call which they seem to produce mainly at mating time. An angry turtle, especially a young one, will often hiss loudly at an attacker.

When trying to attract or impress a female, some males use silent body language to get their message across. Some wave their long toenails in the face of a female, while others have special ways of bobbing their heads.

Diamondback Terrapin

Passing the Time

Like most animals in the wild, turtles spend a good deal of their waking hours looking for food. Some do this mainly at night, others in the daytime, still others at dawn or dusk.

Because turtles cannot control the temperature of their body, most of them also spend as much time as they can basking in the sun. They must do so to warm themselves up after a long swim or a chilly night.

So if you watch carefully when you are near a pond or marsh on a sunny day, you may see a turtle basking on a log or rock with its neck and legs stretched out and its toes spread wide apart to catch as much of the sun's warmth as possible. In fact, you may see several. Sometimes, if good sunning space is scarce, you might even see one turtle sprawled on top of a larger one's shell.

Always room for one more. (Painted Turtles)

Keeping Cool

Turtles can get *too* hot, however, so they must not wander far from water or from trees or rocks. That way, if a turtle feels too hot while sunbathing, it can simply move into the shade. Or it can dunk itself in the water—just as you might if you were lying on the beach.

But if turtles can get too hot, how do the tortoises of the southwestern United States cope with the high temperatures of the desert?

They cope by digging underground burrows. A burrow is much cooler and more moist than the open desert. Deep in the ground, a tortoise can keep cool and save the precious water its body contains. On very hot days the tortoise will probably not come out of its burrow at all.

Tortoises are the only turtles that build any form of home. All other turtles simply make use of the world around them. A sleepy turtle may snooze at the bottom of a marsh, doze under a log or snuggle down into the mud of a pond.

Opposite page:
Snapping Turtle.

35

Sleeping away the Winter

Turtles in northern areas would freeze if they could not find a way to avoid winter. So, like some other animals, they hibernate.

As fall approaches and the weather begins to cool, these turtles start to put on extra fat. This will supply what energy they need through the winter. As the temperature drops still more, they gradually get less and less active. Finally they burrow deep into the mud at the bottom of ponds or into the loose soil of the forest floor and settle in to sleep the winter away.

Scientists have found that the blood of hibernating turtles actually changes to work rather like the antifreeze we buy in winter for our cars. As a result, the turtle's body temperature can drop to only a few degrees above freezing—much lower than that of most animals that hibernate.

In the spring, as the soil or water begins to warm, the turtle's body, too, gradually warms up. Finally the turtle awakens, ready to face another year.

Early warm spells in the winter can be dangerous for turtles. If they wake up too soon from their winter sleep, a return to cold weather may catch them unprepared and they may freeze. In fact, winter can be the biggest danger a turtle faces in its adult life.

Nesting Time

Different types of turtles have their young at different ages. Mud Turtles are about five or six years old when they mate, while the Desert Tortoise must wait until it is about 15 years old. Some turtles nest one or more times a year, others may nest only once every few years. A turtle that nests once a year usually lays its eggs in the spring so that they will be kept warm by the heat of the summer sun.

All turtles bury their eggs in sand or soil. Even the sea turtles come ashore and drag themselves a few hundred metres (yards) onto the beach to lay their eggs.

Many turtles have traditional nesting grounds that have been used for generations. The mother's desire to lay her eggs in a certain place is very strong. This can pose a danger as she will try to cross any barrier including backyards, fences and busy highways to reach her nesting ground. Turtles are sometimes hit by cars as they cross roads on their way to lay their eggs.

Opposite page:

A few kinds of turtles do not have scutes. Instead they have a hard leathery skin over their shell that gives them a sleeker, smooth look. (Softshell Turtle)

As Safe as Mom Can Make Them

The mother turtle usually lays her eggs in the middle of the night. This is the safest time for turtles to be out in the open.

First she digs a hole with her hind feet, using her front legs to hold her body in place. After the hole is dug she holds her body over the nest and deposits her eggs in it.

Depending on the type of turtle, the mother may lay one to several hundred eggs. She then covers the nest and packs down the loose soil with her body. She may pack the soil for quite a distance around the nest. This helps to confuse hungry predators.

This female Snapping Turtle may lay as many as 50 eggs in this hole before she is finished.

On Their Own

The mother never sees her babies.
She leaves her eggs to hatch in the
warmth of the sun. It takes two or
more months for the eggs to
develop. During this time, the
leathery roundish eggs may be
found and eaten by foxes, skunks,
bears, raccoons or other animals.
The nest may also be flooded
during heavy rains and the eggs
washed away, or the eggs may dry
out if they are not buried deep
enough. But most turtle mothers
lay many eggs and this helps
insure that some babies will
survive.

Young Painted Turtle.

The Long Trek

When a baby turtle is ready to hatch, it must break through the tough shell of the egg. To do this, each hatchling has a special tooth called an egg tooth and uses it to slit the egg open. The tooth falls off within a few days.

Once the baby is out of its shell, it climbs up through the soil or sand to the surface. Some lucky hatchlings emerge to find themselves in or very near a suitable place to live. But many young water turtles must now undertake a long journey. Even if they cannot see the water, they know instinctively in which direction to go. One after another they set out across the stretch of sand or through the woods to find the ocean, marsh or pond their mother came from.

This is another dangerous time in the young turtle's life. Hawks, gulls, raccoons, skunks and even fish see the tiny baby turtles as an easy meal. But the babies seem to know this too, and they will usually surface after dark when there is less danger of being spotted by predators.

Opposite page:

Dangerous journey. (Snapping Turtle)

From Small Beginnings

All turtle hatchlings are tiny, about the size of a quarter. It is hard to believe that some of these helpless little turtles may someday grow up to be giant Leatherback Sea Turtles weighing over 700 kilograms (1500 pounds) and measuring nearly 2.5 metres (8 feet) in length. In fact, some Leatherbacks have weighed more than 1000 kilos (2200 pounds)!

The smaller types of turtles may live up to 5 years, but the larger turtles live much longer. There are many stories that tell of amazingly old turtles, but no one is really sure how long turtles can live. After all, when an animal can live for over 100 years it is hard to keep records!

Big or small, turtles are truly amazing creatures. They have survived remarkable changes in the world around them and with their slow-moving life and their built-in armor they will surely be around for generations to come.

Words to Know

Carapace   A turtle's top shell.

Carnivore   An animal that eats mainly meat.

Herbivore   An animal that eats mainly plants.

Hibernate   To go into a deep sleep for the entire winter.

Mate   To come together to produce young.

Musk   A strong smelling substance produced by some animals.

Omnivore   An animal that eats both plants and animals.

Plastron   A turtle's bottom shell.

Scutes   Scaly plates that cover a turtle's shell.

Terrapins   Usually used to describe freshwater turtles.

Tortoise   Turtles that live only on land. (In some countries, however, *tortoise* is commonly used for freshwater turtles as well.)

INDEX

Cover Photo: Bill Ivy

Photo Credits: Robert C. Simpson (Valan Photos), pages 4, 18, 33; Wayne Lankinen (Valan Photos), page 7; J.D. Markou (Valan Photos), pages 8, 45; Bill Ivy, pages 11, 17, 22, 28, 34, 41; James Richards, page 14; Harold Lambert (Miller Services), page 21; Arthur Holbrook (Miller Services), page 25; Wayne Lynch (Master File), page 26; J.D. Taylor (Miller Services), page 30; Brian Morin (Network Stock Photo File), page 38; Robert McCaw (Network Stock Photo File), page 42.

Printed and Bound in Italy by Lego SpA